Faith Working Through Love

Prayers, Meditations and Reflections
Celebrating the Year of Faith

Gareth Byrne

VERITAS

Published 2013 by Veritas Publications
7–8 Lower Abbey Street
Dublin 1, Ireland
publications@veritas.ie
www.veritas.ie

ISBN 978 1 84730 489 6

10 9 8 7 6 5 4 3

A catalogue record for this book is available from the British
Library.

Designed by Heather Costello, Veritas Publications
Printed in the Republic of Ireland by Walsh Colour Print, Co. Kerry

Veritas books are printed on paper made from the wood pulp of
managed forests. For every tree felled, at least one tree is planted,
thereby renewing natural resources.

✳ Introduction: How to Use This Book

Fifty years after the beginning of Vatican II, in the Year of Faith established by Pope Benedict XVI, we reflect on our Christian faith, on all that holds us close to Jesus Christ and through him prompts us to reach out to the world in gratitude and hope. The phrase 'faith working through love' (Galatians 5:6), highlighted in the pope's letter *Porta fidei*, introducing the Year of Faith, sums up the prayers, meditations and reflections found in this book.

Along with well-known and lesser known prayers, you will find in this collection pieces from scripture, passages from the documents of Vatican II and from the *Catechism of the Catholic Church*, as well as relevant sections from the Irish Episcopal Conference's *Share the Good News*: *National Directory for Catechesis in Ireland*. They have been chosen to encourage reflection on the Christian life, the mission of the Church, the call to ministry and the variety of roles we can play in our local Church community. Some pieces emphasise the value of prayer and of continuing reflection and faith development. Other passages highlight the work of justice and peace and that of building up the Christian community together.

This book invites us to recover our appetite for prayer, reflection and mediation on the beauty of God and of God's creation, on our calling to intimacy with God in Christ Jesus and in his Spirit. We are reminded of the gifts we hope to receive and bring to the world, and the mission of love that is the Church:

> Our joy should be to live in the love of God as Jesus has done and to love one another as he has loved us. This is our programme for life.

Share the Good News, 59

This is not a book to be read through, but a series of prompts for prayer and meditation. Take one page at a time or just one phrase perhaps, and reflect on it in the presence of the Lord. Open yourself up to Jesus speaking to you and enter into conversation with him for a moment, for some minutes, for whatever time you may have. Do not be in a rush, but ask the Spirit sent by Christ to encourage you in whatever you need. Stay with the text a while and make it your own. Allow Jesus to draw you to himself and allow yourself to be with him in love. You can do this in a quiet space at home, on a park bench, walking by the sea, before the Blessed Sacrament in your church, or as a focus for prayer with a group of friends. Over a period, go back time and again to the prayers and reflections that nourish you, challenge you, strengthen you, and ask the Holy Spirit to encourage you in making these words come alive in your life.

In this world, with Christ by our side, we too can be gentleness, kindness, generosity, forgiveness, peace, joy and love. If you have found this book helpful, suggest it to those who might enjoy it, to those who are full of hope and those who have no hope at this time. It may be of help to those who are ill, to a friend in need, to anyone who might be open to meeting Christ in a new way.

Each day, we live in Christ's love and bring him with us for others wherever we go.

Share the Good News, 30

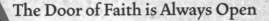

The Door of Faith is Always Open

The 'door of faith' (Acts 14: 27) is always open for us, ushering us into the life of communion with God and offering entry into his Church. It is possible to cross that threshold when the word of God is proclaimed and the heart allows itself to be shaped by transforming grace. To enter through that door is to set out on a journey of a lifetime. It begins with baptism (cf. Romans 6: 4), through which we can address God as Father, and it ends with the passage through death to eternal life, fruit of the resurrection of the Lord Jesus, whose will it was, by the gift of the Holy Spirit, to draw those who believe in him into his own glory (cf. John 17: 22). To profess faith in the Trinity – Father, Son and Holy Spirit – is to believe in one God who is Love (cf. I John 4: 8): the Father, who in the fullness of time sent his Son for our salvation; Jesus Christ, who in the mystery of his death and resurrection redeemed the world; the Holy Spirit, who leads the Church across the centuries as we await the Lord's glorious return.

Benedict XVI, *Porta fidei*, 1

The people of God believes that it is led by the Spirit of the Lord who fills the whole world. Impelled by that faith, they try to discern the true signs of God's presence and purpose in the events, the needs and the desires which it shares with the rest of humanity today. For faith casts a new light on everything and makes known the full ideal which God has set for humanity, thus guiding the mind towards solutions that are fully human.

Vatican II, *Gaudium et spes*, 11

✳

All Creation Sings to the Glory of God

The Christian tradition understands all of creation as the gift of God. God's ongoing creative action includes not only the work of origins but that of salvation and consummation as well. The potential of human nature has been fully revealed in the mystery of Jesus Christ, the Son of God and Son of Mary, risen from the dead. He is the cosmic Christ, Lord over all creation (Philippians 2:5-11). In him all things have been created anew (1 Corinthians 15:45ff). Humankind, our world, all creation, is in need of healing and of wholeness, the salvation in Christ to which he calls all things. Christian spirituality does not seek escape from this world to God. It is rather a way in and with the world to God.

Share the Good News, 14

Creator God,
We have forgotten that you put us in
your world to care for it,
And to sustain it for our children and
our children's children.
We repent of our greed and commit
ourselves to work together,
Even by small steps, to restore your
creation to wholeness. Amen.

Anon

Nicene Creed

I believe in one God,
the Father almighty,
maker of heaven and earth,
of all things visible and invisible.

I believe in one Lord Jesus Christ,
the Only Begotten Son of God,
born of the Father before all ages.
God from God, Light from Light,
true God from true God,
begotten, not made, consubstantial with the
Father;
through him all things were made.
For us men and for our salvation
he came down from heaven,
and by the Holy Spirit was incarnate of the
Virgin Mary,
and became man.

For our sake he was crucified
under Pontius Pilate,
he suffered death and was buried,
and rose again on the third day
in accordance with the Scriptures.
He ascended into heaven
and is seated at the right hand of the Father.

He will come again in glory
to judge the living and the dead
and his kingdom will have no end.

I believe in the Holy Spirit, the Lord, the giver of life,
who proceeds from the Father and the Son,
who with the Father and the Son is adored and glorified,
who has spoken through the prophets.

I believe in one, holy, catholic and apostolic Church.
I confess one Baptism for the forgiveness of sins
and I look forward to the resurrection of the dead
and the life of the world to come. Amen.

I Can Always Talk to God

A first essential setting for learning hope is prayer. When no one listens to me any more, God still listens to me. When I can no longer talk to anyone or call upon anyone, I can always talk to God. When there is no longer anyone to help me deal with a need or expectation that goes beyond the human capacity for hope, he can help me.

Benedict XVI, Spes salvi, 32

Christian prayer has several different forms of expression: adoration, praise, thanksgiving, petition, lament and intercession. It may be entered into in a variety of fashions: vocal prayer expressed outwardly in words, meditation or quiet reflection frequently starting from the Word of God, and contemplation, described by St Teresa of Avila as 'nothing else than a close sharing between friends; it means taking time frequently to be alone with him who we know loves us'.

Share the Good News, 61

Meditation

Meditation is above all a quest. The mind seeks to understand the why and how of the Christian life, in order to adhere and respond to what the Lord is asking. The required attentiveness is difficult to sustain. We are usually helped by books, and Christians do not want for them: the Sacred Scriptures, particularly the Gospels, holy icons, liturgical texts of the day or season, writings of the spiritual fathers, works of spirituality, the great book of creation, and that of history – the page on which the 'today' of God is written ...

Meditation engages thought, imagination, emotion and desire. This mobilisation of faculties is necessary in order to deepen our conviction of faith, prompt the conversion of our heart and strengthen our will to follow Christ. Christian prayer tries above all to meditate on the mysteries of Christ, as in *lectio divina* or in the rosary. This form of prayerful reflection is of great value, but Christian prayer should go further; to knowledge of the love of the Lord Jesus, to union with him.

Catechism of the Catholic Church, 2705, 2708

Contemplation

Contemplative prayer is silence, the 'symbol of the world to come' or 'silent love'. Words in this kind of prayer are not speeches; they are like kindling that feeds the fire of love. In this silence, unbearable to the 'outer' man, the Father speaks to us his incarnate Word, who suffered, died and rose; in this silence the Spirit of adoption enables us to share in the prayer of Jesus.

Catechism of the Catholic Church, 2717

Trust in the Slow Work of God

Above all, trust in the slow work of God.
We are, quite naturally, impatient in everything to reach the end without
delay.
We should like to skip the intermediate stages.
We are impatient of being on the way to something unknown,
something new.
And yet it is the law of all progress that it is made by passing through
some stages of instability
and that it may take a very long time.

And so I think it is with you.
Your ideas mature gradually – let them grow, let them shape themselves
without due haste.
Don't try to force them on, as though you could be today what time
(that is to say grace and circumstances acting on your own goodwill)
will make you tomorrow.

Only God can say what this new spirit gradually forming in you will be.
Give our Lord the benefit of believing that his hand is leading you
and accept the anxiety of leaving yourself in suspense and incomplete.

Pierre Teilhard de Chardin

from God in an Apron

And then suddenly
the One we loved startled us all
He got up from the table
and put on an apron.
Can you imagine how we felt?

God in an apron!

Tenderness encircled us
as he bowed before us.
He knelt and said,
'I chose to wash your feet
because I love you.'

God in an apron, kneeling
I couldn't believe my eyes.
I was embarrassed
until his eyes met mine
I sensed my value then.

He touched my feet
He held them in his strong, brown hands
He washed them.

I can still feel the water
I can still feel the touch of his hands.
I can still see the look in his eyes.

Then he handed me the towel and said,
'As I have done so you must do.'
Learn to bow, learn to kneel.

Let your tenderness encircle
everyone you meet.
Wash their feet
not because *you have to,*
because *you want to.*

Macrina Wiederkehr

United with Him in His Cross and Resurrection

My Lord and my God.

Save us, Saviour of the world,
for by your Cross and Resurrection
you have set us free.

Mystery of Faith Acclamations, after Consecration at Mass

At the altar, we are united with him in his cross and resurrection. The People of God gathered together, participating in the Eucharist through Christ, with him and in him, offer everything they are, too, to God for the good of all humankind.

Share the Good News, 54

The lives of the faithful, their praise, sufferings, prayer and work, are united with Christ and with his total offering, and so acquire a new value.

Catechism of the Catholic Church, 1386

We love because he first loved us.

I John 4: 19

In Communion of Life with Jesus

By faith, the Apostles left everything to follow their master (cf. Mark 10: 28). They believed the words with which he proclaimed the Kingdom of God present and fulfilled in his person (cf. Luke 11: 20). They lived their lives in communion of life with Jesus who instructed them with his teaching, leaving them a new rule of life, by which they would be recognised as his disciples after his death (cf. John 13: 34-35). By faith, they went out to the whole world, following the command to bring the Gospel to all creation (cf. Mark 16: 15) and they fearlessly proclaimed to all the joy of the resurrection, of which they were the faithful witnesses.

By faith, the disciples formed the first community, gathered around the teaching of the Apostles, in prayer, in celebration of the Eucharist, holding their possessions in common so as to meet the needs of the brethren (cf. Acts 2: 42-47) ...

By faith, across the centuries, men and women of all ages, who names are written in the Book of Life (cf. Revelations 7: 9, 13: 8), have confessed the beauty of following the Lord Jesus wherever they were called to bear witness to the fact that they were Christian: in the family, in the workplace, in public life, in the exercise of the charisms and ministries to which they were called.

Benedict XVI, *Porta fidei*, 13

Gospel Living

Traditionally, four signs of commitment, already noted in the Acts of the Apostles as attributes of the early Christian community, have been highlighted as characteristics of gospel living:

* Proclaiming and witnessing to the Gospel message

* Building up a caring Church community based on Gospel values

* Celebrating faith in worship, prayer and through liturgical participation – in communion with God, in Jesus Christ, and with one another

* Service to neighbour, particularly the most poor and most vulnerable, the work of justice.

Share the Good News, 36

They devoted themselves to the apostles' teaching and fellowship, to the breaking of bread and to the prayers. And all who believed were together and had all things in common; and they sold their possessions and goods and distributed them to all, as had any need.

Act of the Apostles 2: 42. 44-45

15

He Continues to Reach Out, Drawing Near to Us

The friends of Jesus became committed to the Lord because they came to know him and his love for them. They saw his commitment to them and to those most in need, his care for the poor, his love for sinners, his ability to change people's lives by his compassionate presence, his challenging stories, his healing words and works. They recognised, too, the most central reality in his life, his close bond to his Father in heaven. He prayed, personally, constantly, intensely, living always in conversation with the One who continually loves the world, and all its people, into life.

Share the Good News, 7

Like so many in the gospel stories, we too have heard Jesus Christ calling us. He continues to reach out, drawing near to us in our own particular places. He is conscious of each person in their need and addresses us personally. This is his way. He has come among us in our humanity and he remains with us always. Of the sick man at Bethzatha he asks with intent: 'Do you want to be well again?' (John 5: 6). He surprises the Samaritan woman at the well, and upsets his companions, when he makes a request of her: 'Give me a drink' (John 4: 7). And to the rich young man, on whom he looks lovingly, he offers an unanswered challenge: 'Come follow me' (Mark 10: 21). Despite our weakness and the inadequacies of our efforts, we too have felt his closeness and known his care. He has touched our very being. As in Galilee two thousand years ago, Jesus Christ offers us now, healing and forgiveness, comfort and challenge, the tenderness and pain of all-embracing love, and a peace in God's presence rooted in commitment to one another and to whole-hearted service of neighbour.

Share the Good News, 1

Communion with Christ and with One Another

'God calls us to become, together, one family, working in common purpose, in communion with God and with one another.

Share the Good News, 26

To follow Christ the perfect human is to become more human oneself.

Vatican II, *Gaudium et spes,* 41

The Church is communion through Christ, with him, and in him. Nothing can bind the faithful together more profoundly than this communion.

Christoph Schönborn

The Eucharist offers us intimate communion with Jesus Christ and committed communion with one another, a tender but radically life-changing embrace. This 'profound encounter with the Lord Jesus' touches us deep within. It transforms our being in his love. And in us he reaches out, in ways often unknown, to offer healing and hope to our wider community and society as a whole.

Share the Good News, 54

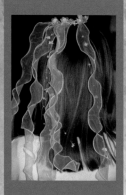

Prayer of the 50th International Eucharistic Congress

Lord Jesus, you were sent by the Father
to gather together those who are scattered.
You came among us, doing good and bringing healing,
announcing the word of salvation
and giving the bread which lasts forever.
Be our companion on life's pilgrim way.

May the Holy Spirit inflame our hearts,
enliven our hope and open our minds,
so that together with our sisters and brothers in faith
we may recognise you in the scriptures
and in the breaking of bread.
May your Holy Spirit transform us
into one body and lead us to walk humbly on the earth,
in justice and love,
as witnesses of your resurrection.

In communion with Mary,
whom you gave us as our Mother,
at the foot of the cross,
through you may all praise, honour and blessing
be to the Father
in the Holy Spirit and in the Church, now and forever.
Amen.

The Most Important Appointment in the Week

Anyone who is really seeking Jesus' friendship responds as often as possible to Jesus' invitation to the feast.

Actually, for a genuine Christian, 'Sunday duty' is just as inappropriate an expression as 'kiss duty' would be to someone who is truly in love. No one can have a living relationship with Christ without going to the place where he is waiting for us. Therefore, from ancient times the celebration of the Mass has been the 'heart of Sunday' and the most important appointment in the week.

YOUCAT: Youth Catechism of the Catholic Church, 219

Take this, all of you, and eat of it,
for this is my Body,
which will be given up for you.

Take this, all of you, and drink from it,
for this is the chalice of my Blood,
the Blood of the new and eternal covenant,
which will be poured out for you and for many
for the forgiveness of sins.

Do this in memory of me.

Words of Consecration at Mass

The 'New' Communion

Jesus replied: Whoever does the will of
God is my brother, and sister, and mother.

Mark 3: 35

On her part, the Church knows that the communion received by her as a gift is destined for all people. Thus the Church feels she owes to each individual and to humanity as a whole the gift received from the Holy Spirit that pours the charity of Jesus Christ into the hearts of believers, as a mystical force for internal cohesion and external growth. The mission of the Church flows from her own nature ... Such a mission has the purpose of making everyone know and live the 'new' communion that the Son of God made man introduced into the history of the world.

John Paul II, *Christifideles laici*, 32

The 50th International Eucharistic Congress Bell

Forgiveness and Reconciliation

Jesus gifted the disciples with peace and joy and sent them as the Father had sent him, to bring forgiveness into the world (John 20:19-23). The Church should be a sign and instrument of that forgiveness and reconciliation. The sacrament of Penance and Reconciliation celebrates Christ's forgiveness of us and his healing of our hearts and minds. By confessing, we take responsibility for our sin, recognising it for what it is. Our sorrow for what we have done, or failed to do, leads us to contrition, absolution, penance and renewed hope. We can act differently, and pledge ourselves so to do. We open ourselves in Jesus Christ to reconciliation with God and with one another.

Share the Good News, 55

Dear brothers and sisters, let us rejoice and be full of confidence. 'We are full of confidence' (2 Corinthians 5:6), as St Paul says to the Corinthians. We are so because the risen Lord is our home and our safety. We do experience limitations and failures in the Church, but the Lord sustains us, healing our wounds and strengthening our love. Let us rejoice in him and be glad! We can rely on the Lord for a new beginning. St Paul gives us the key for any personal or ecclesial renewal: 'We are intent on pleasing Him' (2 Corinthians 5:6). This key to renewal in our lives is a decision to recommit ourselves to love the Lord and to live and to die for him, knowing that His grace will never fail ...

The Irish bell, which resounds from Lough Derg, from Knock and Dublin, must resound in the whole world. Let's ring the bell further through our personal testimony of renewed faith in the Holy Eucharist ...

We are not alone; the Spirit of Pentecost dwells in us. The communion of saints, with Mary at its heart, comes to our assistance as soon as we have rung the bell of prayer in total confidence. Keep hope and be glad, for the kingdom of God is near!

Homily of the Papal Legate, at the 'Statio Orbis' of the 50th International Eucharistic Congress, Dublin, June 2012

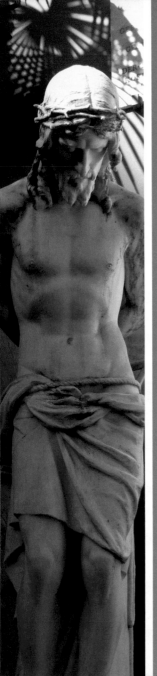

Union with All Those to Whom He Gives Himself

Union with Christ is also union with all those to whom he gives himself. I cannot possess Christ just for myself; I can belong to him only in union with all those who have become, or will become, his own.

Benedict XVI, *Deus caritas est*, 14

His compassion with those who suffer goes so far that he identifies himself with them: 'I was sick and you visited me' (Matthew 25: 36). His preferential love for the sick has not ceased through the centuries to draw the very special attention of Christians toward all who suffer in body and soul. It is the source of tireless efforts to comfort them.

Catechism of the Catholic Church, 1503

The truth of life today and the truth we come to know in the gospel disclose each other, inform each other, build upon each other.

Share the Good News, 63

In migration faith discovers once more the universal message of the prophets, who denounce discrimination, oppression, deportation, dispersion, and persecution as contrary to God's plan. At the same time they proclaim salvation for all, witnessing even in the chaotic events and contradictions of human history, that God continues to work out his plan of salvation until all things are brought together in Christ (see Ephesians 1: 10).

Erga migrantes caritas Christi, 13

Solidarity of the Church with the Whole Human Family

The joys and hopes, the grief and anguish of the people of our time, especially of those who are poor or afflicted, are the joys and hopes, the grief and anguish of the followers of Christ as well. Nothing that is genuinely human fails to find an echo in their hearts. For theirs is a community of people united in Christ and guided by the Holy Spirit in their pilgrimage towards the Father's kingdom, bearers of a message of salvation for all humanity.

Vatican, *Gaudium et spes*, 1

Blessed are the merciful, for they will receive mercy.
Blessed are the pure in heart, for they will see God.
Blessed are the peacemakers, for they will be called children of God.

Matthew 5: 7-9

Come to me all you who are weary and carrying heavy burdens, and I will give you rest. Take my yoke upon you, and learn from me; for I am gentle and humble in heart, and you will find rest for your souls. For my yoke is easy, and my burden is light

Matthew 11: 28-30

Make Me a Channel of Your Peace

Make me a channel of your peace
Where there is hatred let me bring your love
Where there is injury, your pardon Lord
And where there is doubt, true faith in you.

Oh Master grant that I may never seek
So much to be consoled as to console
To be understood as to understand,
To be loved as to love with all my soul.

Make me a channel of your peace
Where there is despair in life, let me bring hope
Where there is darkness, only light,
And where there's sadness, only joy.

Make me a channel of your peace
It is in pardoning that we are pardoned,
In giving to all men that we receive
And in dying that we're born to eternal life.

Sebastian Temple, based on the Prayer of St Frances of Assisi

Suffering Shared

To accept the 'other' who suffers, means that I take up his suffering in such a way that it becomes mine also. Because it has now become a shared suffering, though, in which another person is present, this suffering is penetrated by the light of love. The Latin word *con-solatio*, 'consolation' expresses this beautifully. It suggests *being with* the other in his solitude, so that it ceases to be solitude.

Benedict XVI, *Spe salvi*, 38

My deep personal sharing in the needs and sufferings of others becomes a sharing of my very self with them: if my gift is not to prove a source of humiliation, I must give to others not only something that is my own, but my very self; I must be personally present in my gift.

Benedict XVI, *Deus caritas est*, 34

Blessing Prayer for Healing

May you desire to be healed.
May what is wounded in your life be restored to good health.
May you be receptive to the ways in which healing needs to happen.
May you take good care of yourself.
May you extend compassion to all that hurts within your body, mind, spirit.
May you be patient with the time it takes to heal.
May you be aware of the wonders of your body, mind and spirit and their amazing capacity to heal.
May you be open to receive from those who extend kindness, care and compassion to you.
May you rest peacefully under the sheltering wings of divine love, trusting in this gracious presence.
May you find little moments of beauty and joy to sustain you.
May you keep hope in your heart.

Joyce Rupp

The Holy Spirit, Our Guide

Prompted by the Holy Spirit, we seek to live our faith in Jesus Christ and become the supportive and unified community of disciples he calls us to be. We are convinced that knowing Christ's love for us can change our lives, convert our hearts and transform our world.

Share the Good News, 1

The Spirit helps us in our weakness; for we do not know how to pray as we ought, but the Spirit himself intercedes for us with sighs too deep for words.

Romans 8: 26

The tradition that comes from the apostles makes progress in the Church, with the help of the Holy Spirit. There is a growth in insight into the realities and words that are being passed on. This comes about through the contemplation and study of believers who ponder these things in their hearts (see Luke 2:19).

Vatican II, *Dei verbum*, 8

Come O Holy Spirit

Come Holy Spirit, fill the hearts of your faithful.
And kindle in them the fire of your love.
Send forth your Spirit and they shall be created.
And you will renew the face of the earth.

O God, by the light of the Holy Spirit you have taught the hearts of the faithful.
In the same Spirit, help us to know what is truly right and always rejoice in your consolation.
We ask this through Christ, our Lord. Amen.

The Liberating, Saving and Loving Word of God

The Church interprets the Word of God in the particular context of each new generation. Together we seek to transform human life in the power of God's love made known abundantly in Jesus Christ. We seek to confirm our capacity for love also revealed to us fully in Jesus Christ.

Share the Good News, 27

When our understanding of humanity is based in relationship with God and with one another, we will be open to hear the liberating, saving and loving Word of God.

Share the Good News, 28

The study of Scripture requires not only an historical exegesis, using serious historical research methods, but also a theological exegesis that reflects on the spirit in which the text was written and on how it has come to be understood in the Church. As Pope Benedict has pointed out: 'every text must be read and interpreted keeping in mind the unity of the whole of Scripture, the living tradition of the Church and the light of faith.'

Share the Good News, 47

Encountering God's Thirst for Us

The wonder of prayer is revealed beside the well where we come seeking water: there, Christ comes to meet every human being. It is he who first seeks us and asks us for a drink. Jesus thirsts; his asking arises from the depths of God's desire for us. Whether we realise it or not, prayer is the encounter of God's thirst with ours. God thirsts that we may thirst for him.

Catechism of the Catholic Church, 2560

In Jesus of Nazareth, we see the person we are called to become.
In Jesus of Nazareth, we see how God has committed himself to us.
In Jesus of Nazareth, we see how we can completely belong to God.
In Jesus of Nazareth, we see how much freedom and humanity, how much courage and self-forgetfulness a person can possess.
In Jesus of Nazareth, we see that there is a future for each one of us.

Anon

The Lord's Prayer

Our Father
Who art in heaven
Hallowed be thy name
Thy kingdom come
Thy will be done
On earth as it is in heaven
Give us this day our daily bread
And forgive us our trespasses
As we forgive those who trespass
against us
And lead us not into temptation
But deliver us from evil.
Amen.

An Phaidir

Ár nAthair atá ar neamh,
go naofar d'ainm.
Go dtaga do ríocht,
go ndéantar do thoil ar an talamh
mar a dhéantar ar neamh.
Ár n-arán laethúil tabhair dúinn
inniú,
agus maith dúinn ár bhfiacha,
mar a mhaithimidne dár bhféichiúna
féin.
Agus ná lig sinn i gcathú,
ach soar sinn ó olc.
Áiméan.

Jesus taught his disciples to pray by asking the Heavenly Father not for 'my' but for 'our' daily bread. Thus, he desired every person to feel co-responsible for his brothers so that no one would want for what he needs in order to live. The earth's produce forms a gift which God has destined 'for the entire human family'.

Benedict XVI, Angelus, St Peter's Square, 12 Nov 2006

Diversity of Ministry, Unity of Mission

In the Church not everyone walks along the same path, yet all are called to holiness and have obtained an equal privilege of faith through the justice of God (see 2 Peter 1:1) ... all the faithful enjoy a true equality with regard to the dignity and the activity which they share in the building up of the body of Christ.

Vatican II, *Lumen gentium*, 32

In the church there is diversity of ministry but unity of mission.

Vatican II, *Apostolicam actuositatem*, 2

We are called to bring the values and demands of the gospel into every sphere of our human life and activity. Each day, we live in Christ's love and bring him with us for others wherever we go. We have a gift with which to gift others – Jesus Christ. 'The community must always be fully prepared in the pursuit of its apostolic vocation to give help to those who are searching for Christ.'

Share the Good News, 48

Close collaboration and coordination of all the apostolic works under the direction of the bishop should be promoted in the diocese as a whole or in its different parts. Thus, all the undertakings and organisations, whether their object be catechetical, missionary, charitable, social, familial, educational, or any other pastoral purpose, will act in harmony, and the unity of the diocese will be more clearly evident.

Vatican II, *Christus Dominus*, 17

The Love that Flows from Christ

Whoever loves Christ loves the Church, and desires the Church to be increasingly the image and instrument of the love that flows from Christ.

Benedict XVI, *Deus caritas est*, 33

Dearest Jesus, teach me to be generous:
teach me to love and serve you as you deserve;
to give and not to count the cost;
to fight and not to heed the wounds;
to toil and not to seek for rest;
to labour and to look for no reward,
save that of knowing that I do your holy will.

Prayer of St Ignatius

The Lord is my Shepherd

The Lord is my shepherd;
there is nothing I shall want.
Fresh and green are the pastures
where he gives me repose.
Near restful waters he leads me,
to revive my drooping spirit.

He guides me along the right path;
he is true to his name
If I should walk in the valley of
darkness
no evil would I fear.
You are there with your crook and
your staff;
with these you give me comfort.

You have prepared a banquet for me
in the sight of my foes.
My head you have anointed with oil;
my cup is overflowing.

Surely goodness and kindness shall
follow me
all the days of my life.
In the Lord's own house shall I dwell
for ever and ever.

Psalm 22

The Parish: A Community of Love

The parish offers an outstanding example of community apostolate, for it gathers into one all the human diversities that are to be found there and inserts them into the universality of the church. The laity should develop the habit of working in the parish in close cooperation with their priests, of bringing before the ecclesial community their own problems, world problems, and questions regarding humanity's salvation, to examine them together and solve them by general discussion.

Vatican II, *Apostolicam actuositatem*, 10

✳

We always want a God who is going to fix our problems, but God is saying, 'I'll give you the strength so you become one of those who work with others to bring peace to our world ...' It's up to you and me, but God will give us strength ... God trusts us so much; God wants us to become men and women who can receive forgiveness and give forgiveness, who can receive wisdom and give wisdom. Jesus kneeling before his disciples is a revelation of Jesus kneeling at our feet saying 'I trust you, I believe in you, I love you' and calling us to stand up and work for love.

Jean Vanier

Training for the apostolate cannot consist only in being taught theory; on that account there is need, right from the start of training, to learn gradually and prudently to see things in the light of faith, to judge and act always in its light, to improve and perfect oneself by working with others, and in this way to enter actively into the service of the Church.

Vatican II, *Apostolicam actuositatem*, 29

Contributing to the Christian Community

Various types of ministry are necessary for the implanting and growth of the Christian community, and once they have been called forth from the body of the faithful, by the divine call, they are to be carefully fostered and nurtured by all. Among these functions are those of priests, deacons and catechists ... Religious brothers and sisters, likewise, play an indispensable role in planting and strengthening the kingdom of Christ in souls, and in the work of further extending it, both by their prayers and active work.

Vatican II, *Ad gentes divinitus*, 5

Through priests, despite their human frailty, Jesus continues to teach, sanctify and build up the community of the faithful. Through them, the Church continues to experience the loving kindness and forgiveness of Christ and to respond to that love in worship, praise and thanksgiving.

Share the Good News, 56

Pastors, however, should recognise and promote the dignity and responsibility of the laity in the Church... Many benefits for the church are to be expected from this familiar relationship between laity and the pastors. The laity's sense of their own responsibility is strengthened, their zeal is encouraged, they are more ready to add their strengths to the work of the pastors.

Vatican II, *Lumen gentium*, 37

It Helps, Now and Then, to Step Back and Take the Long View

It helps now and then, to step back and take the long view.
The kingdom is not only beyond our efforts, it is beyond our vision.
We accomplish in our lifetime only a tiny fraction of the magnificent enterprise that is God's work.
Nothing we do is complete, which is a way of saying that the kingdom is always beyond us.
No statement says all that could be said.
No prayer fully expresses our faith.
No confession brings perfection.
No pastoral visit brings wholeness.
No programme accomplishes the Church's mission.
No set of goals and objectives includes everything.
This then is what we are about.
We plant the seed that one day will grow.
We water seeds already planted, knowing that the future holds promise.
We lay foundations that will need further development.
We provide yeast that produces far beyond our capabilities.
We cannot do everything, and there is a sense of liberation in realising that.
This enables us to do something and to do it well.
It may be incomplete, but it is a beginning, a step along the way,
an opportunity for the Lord's grace to enter and do the rest.
We may never see the end results,
but that is the difference between the master builder and the worker.
We are workers, not master builders; ministers not messiahs.
We are prophets of a future not our own.

Attributed to Oscar Romero

Together Building up the Church

Gathered together as the people of God and established in the one body of Christ under one head, the laity, whoever they are, are called as living members to apply to the building up of the Church and to its continual sanctification all the powers which they received from the goodness of the Creator and from the grace of the redeemer. The apostolate of the laity is a sharing in the Church's saving power.

Vatican II, *Lumen gentium*, 33

Each individual lay person must be a witness before the world to the resurrection and life of the Lord Jesus, and a sign of the living God.

Vatican II, *Lumen gentium*, 38

It is therefore quite clear that all Christians in whatever state or walk of life are called to the fullness of life and to the perfection of charity, and this holiness is conducive to a more human way of living even in society here on earth. In order to reach this perfection the faithful should use the strength dealt to them by Christ's gift, so that following in his footsteps and conformed to his image, doing the will of God in everything, they may wholeheartedly devote themselves to the glory of God and to the service of their neighbour.

Vatican II, *Lumen gentium*, 40

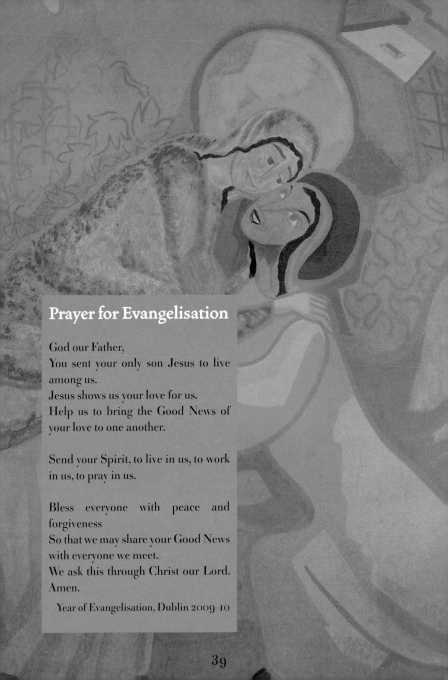

Prayer for Evangelisation

God our Father,
You sent your only son Jesus to live among us.
Jesus shows us your love for us.
Help us to bring the Good News of your love to one another.

Send your Spirit, to live in us, to work in us, to pray in us.

Bless everyone with peace and forgiveness
So that we may share your Good News with everyone we meet.
We ask this through Christ our Lord.
Amen.

Year of Evangelisation, Dublin 2009-10

Co-responsibility for the Church's Being and Action

Now there are varieties of gifts, but the same Spirit; and there are varieties of service, but the same Lord; and there are varieties of working, but it is the same God who inspires them all in everyone. To each is given the manifestation of the Spirit for the common good.

1 Corinthians 12: 4-7

It is necessary to improve pastoral structures in such a way that the co-responsibility of all the members of the People of God in their entirety is gradually promoted, with respect for vocations and for the respective roles of the consecrated and of lay people.

This demands a change in the mindset, particularly concerning lay people. They must no longer be viewed as 'collaborators' of the clergy but truly recognised as 'co-responsible', for the Church's being and action, thereby fostering the consolidation of a mature and committed laity.

Benedict XVI, *Address to the Pastoral Convention of the Diocese of Rome*, 26 May 2009

Live Out Your Responsibility

Don't be afraid then
that your obedience to the gospel,
your listening to others,
will impoverish your personality
or decrease your responsibility.
It summons you rather
to live out your responsibility
in your encounter with others.

Rule for a New Brother

Let love be genuine; hate what is evil, hold fast to what is good; love one another with mutual affection; outdo one another in showing honour. Do not lag in zeal, be ardent in the spirit, serve the Lord. Rejoice in hope, be patient in suffering, persevere in prayer. Contribute to the needs of the saints; extend hospitality to strangers.

Bless those who persecute you; bless and do not curse them. Rejoice with those who rejoice, weep with those who weep. Live in harmony with one another ... If it is possible, so far as it depends on you, live peaceably with all.

Romans: 12: 9-18

Inclusion begins in our hearts. It begins with love. We can open our hearts to one another and recognise the strengths of every person. When each person is allowed to share their gifts our community is strengthened.

It's My Church Too!

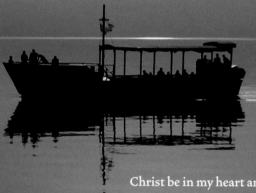

St Patrick's Breastplate

Christ be near at either hand,
Christ behind before me stand,
Christ with me where e'er I go,
Christ around above below.

Christ be in my heart and mind,
Christ within my soul enshrined,
Christ control my wayward heart;
Christ abide and ne'er depart.

Prompted by the Love of Jesus Christ

'Whatever you are doing, whether speaking or acting, do everything in the name of the Lord Jesus Christ, giving thanks to God the Father through him' (Colossians 3: 17).

A life like this calls for a continuous exercise of faith, hope and charity. Only the light of faith and meditation on the word of God can enable us to find everywhere and always the God 'in whom we live and exist' (Acts 17: 28); only thus can we seek his will in everything, see Christ in everyone, acquaintance or stranger, make sound judgements on the true meaning and value of temporal realities both in themselves and in relation to our final end...

Divine love 'poured into our hearts by the Holy Spirit who has been given to us' (Romans 5: 5), enables lay people to express concretely in their lives the spirit of the Beatitudes. Following Jesus in his poverty, want does not depress them, nor is plenty a cause of pride. Imitating the humble Christ, they do not long for empty glory (see Galatians 5: 26).

Vatican II, *Apostolicam actuositatem*, 4

Be a Gardener.
Dig a ditch.
Toil and sweat.
And turn the earth upside down.
And seek the deepness.
And water plants in time.
Continue this labour.
And make sweet floods to run,
and noble and abundant fruits
to spring.
Take this food and drink,
and carry it to God as your true
worship.

Julian of Norwich

The Servant Song

Chorus:
Will you let me be your servant,
Let me be as Christ to you.
Pray that I may have the grace to,
Let you be my servant too.

We are pilgrims on a journey, we
are trav'llers on the road,
We are here to help each other,
walk the mile and bear the load.

Chorus

I will hold the Christ-light for
you, in the night-time of your
fear.
I will hold my hand out to you,
speak the peace you long to hear.

Chorus

I will weep when you are
weeping. When you laugh, I'll
laugh with you.
I will share your joy and sorrow,
'til we've seen this journey
through.

Chorus

When we sing to God in heaven,
we shall find such harmony.
Born of all we've known
together, of Christ's love and
agony.

Chorus

Richard Gillard

44

Prayer to St Laurence O'Toole

St Laurence O'Toole, man of faith, you were in the middle of family and political conflict from your earliest days. Give the gift of peace and hope to all who experience the trauma of division in families, in communities and among nations.

St Laurence O'Toole, man of faith, you recognised the call to serve the Lord in a particular way at Glendalough. Give the gift of perseverance to all who are discerning their Christian vocation at this time.

St Laurence O'Toole, man of faith, you had the openness to accept a position of leadership in your community at an early age. Bless young people with a spirit of generosity to offer themselves in the service of the gospel.

St Laurence O'Toole, man of faith, you inspired people by your commitment to the spiritual life and the recitation of the prayer of the Church. Fill us with that desire to pray in communion with each other throughout the day.

St Laurence O'Toole, man of faith, you opened your heart and your doors to those who were poor. Increase our awareness of those in need and inspire us to act with justice and charity at all times.

St Laurence O'Toole, man of faith, you were respected for your commitment to the Church and to your country. Grant us the grace to live in this world while always reflecting the eternal values of the Kingdom.

St Laurence O'Toole, man of faith, you gave your last ounce of energy in the cause of peace. Give us the gift of tirelessness as we try to live as instruments of Christ's peace, love and tolerance.
Amen.

Dublin Diocese, Year of Faith, 2012–13

Openness to God's Innermost Secret

God's very being is love. By sending his only Son and the Spirit of Love in the fullness of time, God has revealed his innermost secret. God himself is an eternal exchange of love, Father, Son and Holy Spirit, and he has destined us to share in that exchange.

Catechism of the Catholic Church, 221

Without God man neither knows which way to go, nor even understands who he is ...
Openness to God makes us open towards our brothers and sisters and towards an understanding of life as a joyful task to be accomplished in a spirit of solidarity ...
God's love calls us to move beyond the limited and the ephemeral, it gives us courage to continue seeking and working for the benefit of all.

Benedict XVI, *Caritas in veritate*, 78

When one falls in love, life becomes suffused with new colour, new life, new energy, new hope. All this is experienced as unexpected and unmerited gift. Some are content to revel in the gift, aware now that life is far richer and deeper than they had realised. Others experience the Giver in the gift; they sense that what they have been given is a share in a divine love which can permeate and renew this broken world.

Donal Dorr

Tenderness and Strength

Healing is always tender, but tenderness does not mean sentimentality and a show of emotion. Rather it is unearthing gentleness and kindness, which shows another person that we consider them important and precious. Tenderness is revealed through gesture and tone of voice. It is not weakness, but a reassuring strength, transmitted through the eyes and the body. It is revealed in the attitude of the one, completely attentive to the other. It does not impose itself; it is not aggressive; it is gentle and humble. It does not issue orders.

Much of our capacity to heal another depends on our state of mind. Being able to listen is one of the greatest gifts that we can offer one another. To listen and hear, we have to be aware of the chattering that goes on in our minds, judging, thinking, evaluating, leaping in, taking things personally, being bored, being distracted, reacting – these are all part of everybody's life. Sometimes we are so scattered that we are not even aware that we are not present, that we are using our minds to try and solve some other problem, that we are only half listening.

Sr Stanislaus Kennedy

The Richness of the Human Condition

The Church as a community of faith can benefit from the richness of the human condition, learning from the diversity of gifts given and callings experienced, and, in the words of Pope Paul VI, 'find again greater light, new energy and fuller joy in the fulfilment of her own mission'.

Share the Good News, 113

The dignity of the human person demands that justice and solidarity be recognised as key dimensions of all catechetical efforts. It is especially important that we draw into this dialogue of faith and learn from those who have sometimes been forgotten or isolated or treated as outsiders for whatever reason.

Share the Good News, 112

Let the peace of Christ rule in your hearts, to which indeed you were called in the one body. And be thankful. Let the word of Christ dwell in you richly.

Colossians 3: 15-16a

Choose Life: Prayer for the Child in the Womb

Lord Jesus, you are the source and lover of life.
Reawaken in us respect for every human life.

Help us to see in each child the marvellous work of our Creator.
Open our hearts to welcome every child as a unique and wonderful gift.

Guide the work of doctors, nurses and midwives.
May the life of a mother and her baby in the
womb be equally cherished and respected.

Help those who make our laws to uphold the
uniqueness and sacredness of every human life,
from the first moment of conception to natural death.

Give us wisdom and generosity to build a society that cares for all.

Together with Mary, your Mother,
In whose womb you took on our human nature,
Help us to choose life in every decision we take.

We ask this in the joyful hope of eternal life
with you, and in the communion of the Blessed Trinity.
Amen.

Irish Catholic Bishops' Conference

Choosing to Have Your Child Baptised

Choosing to have your child baptised is ... a significant decision, not to be taken lightly. A full conversation should take place between parents/guardians, the wider family and with parish leaders. The integrity of the sacrament must be respected, while the desire of the parents/guardians to baptise their child should also be encouraged. This requires careful discussion before a decision to baptise is finalised.

Share the Good News, 92

Godparents and grandparents should be encouraged in their role of supporting the parents in the faith formation of their children. Family and parish support for parents/guardians, godparents and grandparents as they foster the human and spiritual growth of their child is essential.

Share the Good News, 92

The Family, the First Community

The primary place of encounter with God for most adults, and children, is family life. For Christians the family is the first experience of Church.

Share the Good News, 82

It rests with parents to prepare their children from an early age, within the family circle, to discern God's love for everyone; they will teach them little by little – and above all by their example – to be concerned about their neighbours' needs, material and spiritual. The whole family, accordingly, and its community life should be a kind of apprenticeship to the apostolate.

Vatican II, *Apostolicam actuositatem*, 30

As we live through the different stages of family life, we never stop learning. As we endeavour to pass on our faith to children and grandchildren, we learn in new ways too.

Share the Good News, 82

Children, Living Witnesses of Christ's Love

Children too have an apostolate of their own. In their own measure they are true living witnesses of Christ among their companions.

Vatican II, *Apostolicam actuositatem*, 12

Sharing faith with the young is the work of the whole Christian community, a responsibility it is happy to undertake and to invest its energy in. Adult Catholics recognise that in this conversation, children, too, can be an inspiration to them opening adults to fresh ways of seeing life, love and relationships, with one another and with God and thereby, coming to understand their own faith anew.

Share the Good News, 91

Children's Creed

I believe that God is my Father in heaven.
I believe he made the world.
That he gives me life.
That he helps me grow.
I believe that Jesus is the Son of God and the Son of Mary.
Jesus shows me that God is Love.
Jesus lived and died for me.
Jesus is alive, alive in me and in my neighbour.
I believe in the Holy Spirit.
Who helps me love others.
Who makes me holy.
Who helps me to know God better.
I believe in God's family, the Church.
I believe that I will be happy with God forever and ever.
Amen.

Anon

Young People as Active Subjects

Young people cannot be considered only objects of catechesis, but also active subjects and protagonists of evangelisation and artisans of social renewal.

General Directory for Catechesis, 183

The young should become the first apostles of the young, in direct contact with them, exercising the apostolate by themselves among themselves, taking account of their social environment.

Vatican II, *Apostolicam actuositatem*, 12

Lord I know that you love me and that you have great plans for me. But sometimes I am overwhelmed by the thoughts of my future. Show me how to walk forward one day at a time.

As I explore the various options which lie before me, help me to listen openly to others, and pay attention to what is in the depths of my own heart. In this way, may I hear your call to a way of life which allows me to love as only I can, and allow me to serve others with the special gifts you have given to me.
Amen.

Anon

Heaven is Wherever God Is

Heaven is wherever God is. The word 'heaven' does not designate a place but, rather, indicates God's presence, which is not bound by time and space. We should not look for heaven in the clouds. Wherever we turn to God in his glory and to our neighbour in his need; wherever we experience the joys of love; whenever we convert and allow ourselves to be reconciled with God, *heaven opens there*.

YOUCAT, 518

Cry out with joy to the Lord, all the earth.
Serve the Lord with gladness.
Come before him singing for joy.

Know that he, the Lord, is God.
He made us we belong to him,
we are his people, the sheep of his flock.

Indeed, how good is the Lord,
eternal his merciful love.
He is faithful from age to age.

Psalm 99

Dialogue in the World

Catholics must be ready to collaborate with all men and women of good will in the promotion of all that is true, just, holy, all that is worthy of love (see Philippians 4: 8). They are to enter into dialogue with them with understanding and courtesy, and are to search for means of improving social and public institutions along the lines of the gospel.

Vatican II, *Apostolicam actuositatem*, 14

From the family circle to the international realm, may each person feel and be *co-responsible for building peace*.

John Paul II, General Audience,
Ash Wednesday, 5 Mar, 2003

Those who practice charity in the Church's name will never seek to impose the Church's faith upon others. They realise that a pure and generous love is the best witness to the God in whom we believe and by whom we are driven to love.

Benedict XVI, *Deus caritas est*, 31

Speak in such a way
that you can still hear what the other is saying,
and that he will still be ready to hear you.
Whether you speak or keep silent
let it proceed from the peace of the Lord.

Rule for a New Brother

Listening as Spiritual Hospitality

To listen is very hard,
Because it asks of us so much interior stability
that we no longer need to prove ourselves by
speeches, arguments, statements or declarations.
True listeners no longer have an inner need
to make their presence known.
They feel free to receive, to welcome, to accept.
Listening is much more than allowing another to talk
while waiting for a chance to respond.
Listening is paying full attention to others
and welcoming them into our very beings.
The beauty of listening is that,
those who are listened to start feeling accepted,
start taking their words more seriously
and discovering their own true selves.
Listening is a form of spiritual hospitality
by which you invite strangers to become friends,
to get to know your inner selves more fully,
and even to dare to be silent with you.

Henri Nouwen

We cannot truly pray to God the Father of all if we
treat any people as other than sisters and brothers,
for all are created in God's image. People's relation to
God the Father and their relation to women and men
are so dependent on each other that the scripture says
'they who do not love, do not know God' (1 John 4: 8).

Vatican II, Nostra aetate, 5

The Angelus

The Angel of the Lord declared unto Mary
and she conceived by the Holy Spirit
Hail Mary, full of grace,
the Lord is with thee.
Blessed art thou among women
and blessed is the fruit of thy womb, Jesus.
Holy Mary, Mother of God,
pray for us sinners,
now and at the hour of our death. Amen.
Behold the handmaid of the Lord.
Be it done unto me according to your Word.
Hail Mary ...
And the Word was made flesh
and dwelt among us.
Hail Mary ...
Pray for us, O holy Mother of God,
that we may be made worthy of the promises of Christ.

Let us pray.
Pour forth, we beseech you O Lord, your grace into our hearts: that we, to
whom the Incarnation of Christ your Son was made known by the message
of an Angel, may by his Passion and Cross be brought to the glory of his
Resurrection,
Through the same Christ our Lord.
Amen.

Woman of Faith, Woman of Hope, Woman of Love

The community of Christ is deeply conscious of the presence of Mary in its midst and at its centre. The whole of her life, graced from beginning to end, is recognised as a faith-filled response to God's call, saying 'yes' and giving 'Life to the world'. The Mother of Jesus, the Mother of the Son of God, having accepted a new mission from Jesus on the Cross, is embraced, too, as our mother, the mother of all believers, the Mother of the Church. She is fully human, 'a woman of strength, who experienced poverty, suffering, flight and exile', the first disciple, sharing with all other human persons the need for salvation in Christ. Mary continues to inspire the women and men of today, becoming herself a symbol of hope for the pilgrim Church's life on earth. Woman of faith, woman of hope, woman of love, completely at home with the Word of God; we have experienced the gift of her goodness, the unfailing love that she pours out from the depths of her heart. With Mary, who receives the Word, embodies the Word and lives the Word, the Church also receives, embodies and witnesses to the Word of God, day by day.

Share the Good News, 27

Share the Good News
Litany of Our Lady

Mary, mother of Christ,
pray for us.
Mary, mother of God,
pray for us.
Mary, mother of the Church,
pray for us.
Mary, our mother,
pray for us.
Mary, Queen of Ireland,
pray for us.
Mary, Queen of Peace,
pray for us

Share the Good News, 173

I Have My Mission

God has created me to do Him some definite service; He has committed some work to me which He has not committed to another.

I have my mission – I never may know it in this life, but I shall be told it in the next ...

I am a link in a chain, a bond of connection between persons.

He has not created me for naught. I shall do good, I shall do His work;

I shall be an angel of peace, a preacher of truth in my own place, while not intending it, if I do but keep His commandments.

Therefore I will trust Him. Whatever, wherever I am, I can never be thrown away.

If I am in sickness, my sickness may serve Him; in perplexity, my perplexity may serve Him ...

He does nothing in vain ... He knows what He is about.

He may take away my friends, He may throw me among strangers,

He may make me feel desolate, make my spirit sink, hide my future from me – still He knows what He is about.

Blessed John Henry Newman

Do Not Worry

Look at the birds of the air; they neither sow nor reap nor gather into barns, and yet your heavenly Father feeds them. Are you not more valuable than they? And can any of you by worrying add a single hour to your span of life? And why do you worry about clothing? Consider the lilies of the field, how they grow, they neither toil nor spin, yet I tell you even Solomon in all his glory was not clothed like one of these. But if God so clothes the grass of the field, which is alive today and tomorrow is thrown into the oven, will he not much more clothe you – you of little faith? Therefore do not worry, saying 'What will we eat?' or 'What will we wear?' For it is the Gentiles who strive for all these things; and indeed your heavenly Father knows that you need all these things. But strive first for the kingdom of God and his righteousness, and all these things will be given to you as well.

Matthew 6: 26-33

Every day has enough trouble of its own.
When you go to sleep,
bury all that has happened in the mercy of God.
It will be safe there.
Stand back from what has happened,
and be grateful for it all.

When the new day begins
be sure that you yourself can be
new and pure as new light.
It is like the resurrection.

Rule for a New Brother

At Least at Night

At least at night
let your heart
have a rest
At least at night
stop your career,
calm those desires
that nearly madden you,
see if you can manage
to put your dreams to sleep.
Yield yourself,
body and soul,
yield yourself
really,
truly and completely
into God's hands!

Dom Hélder Câmara

> When at last I cling to you with
> all my being, for me there will
> be no more sorrow, no more
> toil. Then at last I shall be alive
> with true life, for my life will be
> wholly filled with you.

St Augustine, *Confessions*, Book X, 28

Night Prayer, Canticle of Simeon

Save us Lord while we are awake;
protect us while we sleep;
that we may keep watch with Christ
and rest with him in peace.

At last all powerful Master
you give leave to your servant
to go in peace, according to your
promise.

For my eyes have seen your salvation
which you have prepared for all
nations,
the light to enlighten the Gentiles
and give glory to Israel, your people.

Glory be to the Father
and to the Son,
and to the Holy Spirit.
As it was in the beginning,
is now and ever shall be,
world without end.
Amen.

Save us Lord while we are awake;
Protect us while we sleep;
That we may keep watch with Christ
and rest with him in peace.

Luke 2: 29-32

Prayer of Abandonment

Father,
I abandon myself into your hands; do
with me what you will.
Whatever you may do, I thank you:
I am ready for all, I accept all.
Let only your will be done in me, and in
all your creatures.
I wish no more than this, O Lord.
Into your hands I commend my soul.
I offer it to you with all the love of my heart,
For I love you Lord,
and so need to give myself,
to surrender myself into your hands,
without reserve,
and with boundless confidence,
for you are my Father.
Amen.

Blessed Charles de Foucauld

The Lord is Very Near

Rejoice in the Lord always; again I will say, rejoice. Let your gentleness
be known to everyone. The Lord is near. Do not worry about anything,
but in everything by prayer and supplication with thanksgiving let your
requests be made known to God. And the peace of God, which surpasses
all understanding, will guard your hearts and your minds in Christ Jesus.

Finally, beloved, whatever is true, whatever is honourable, whatever is just,
whatever is pure, whatever is pleasing, whatever is commendable, if there
is any excellence and if there is anything worthy of praise, think about these
things ... and the God of peace will be with you.

Philippians 4: 4-9

Acknowledgements

p. 11 Pierre Teilhard de Chardin, *Hearts on Fire: Praying with Jesuits*, Michael Harter, trans., St Louis, MO: The Institute of Jesuit Scholars, 1993, pp. 102–3.

p. 12 Macrina Wiederkehr, 'God in an Apron', *Seasons of Your Heart: Prayer and Reflections, Revised and Expanded*, New York: HarperOne, 1991, p. 79.

p. 17 Christoph Schönborn, *Living the Catechism of the Catholic Church: The Creed*, San Francisco: Ignatius Press, 1995, p. 134.

p. 26 Joyce Rupp, 'Blessing Prayer for Healing', *Out of the Ordinary: Prayers, Poems and Reflections for Every Season*, Notre Dame, IN: Ave Maria Press, 2000. Used with permission of the publishers, Ave Maria Press, Inc., PO Box 428, Notre Dame, Indiana 46556, www.avemariapress.com.

p. 35 Jean Vanier, *Encountering 'the Other'*, Mahwah, NJ: Paulist Press, 2006, pp. 60–1.

p. 41 *Rule for a New Brother*, Springfield, IL: Templegate Publishers, 1997, p. 20.

p. 41 Dublin Jubilee–AD 2000 Office, *It's My Church Too! The Inclusion of People with a Disability in the Life of the Church*, Dublin, 2000, p. 14.

p. 44 Richard Gillard, 'The Servant Song' © 1997 Scripture in Song, a division of Integrity Music, Inc. Used by permission. All rights reserved.

pp. 44–5 Icon of St Laurence O'Toole written by Mihai Cucu. Commissioned by the Archdiocese of Dublin for the Year of Faith 2012–13. Copyright Archdiocese of Dublin.

p. 46 Donal Dorr, *Divine Energy: God Beyond Us, Within Us, Among Us*, Liguori, MO: Liguori Publications, 1996.

p. 47 Sr Stanislaus Kennedy, *Now is the Time: Spiritual Reflections*, Dublin: TownHouse, 1998, p. 96.

p. 54 *Rule for a New Brother*, p. 12.

p. 55 Henri Nouwen, *Bread for the Journey: A Daybook of Wisdom and Faith*, New York: HarperCollins, 1997, reflection for 11th March.

p. 58 Blessed John Henry Newman, *Meditations and Devotions*, London: Longmans, Green, 1907, pp. 301-2.

p. 59 *Rule for a New Brother*, p. 54.

p. 60 Dom Hélder Câmara, 'At Least at Night', *A Thousand Reasons for Living*, London: Darton, Longman & Todd, 1981.

p. 61 Blessed Charles de Foucauld, *Charles de Foucauld*, Robert Ellsberg, ed., New York: Orbis, 1999, p. 102.

Catechism of the Catholic Church, Dublin: Veritas, 1994.
© Veritas-Libreria Editrice Vaticana.

Irish Episcopal Conference, *Share the Good News: National Directory for Catechesis in Ireland*, Dublin: Veritas Publications, 2010.

YOUCAT: Youth Catechism of the Catholic Church, San Francisco: Ignatius Press, 2011.

Cover image: Parish Church of Sant Vicenç, Tossa del Mar, Catalonia.

All photographs © Gareth Byrne.